In Search
of Chopin's Poland

In Search of Chopin's Poland

Text by

Pamela & Iwo Załuski

Photographs by

Hanna & Juliusz Komarnicki

Ars Polona · Warsaw

Cover and Graphics Designer
Paweł Kamiński

Photographs on pages 79, 80, 104, 105, 115, 117, 120
come from archives of Wydawnictwo „Wiedza i Życie" S.A., Warsaw

Copyright © Ars Polona, Warsaw, Poland 1999

Photograph on page 3:
Fryderyk Chopin (1829) Reproduction of an oil painting by Ambroży Mieroszewski.
Original lost. Property of Photo Library, Chopin Society, Warsaw.

ISBN 83-87682-19-5

Printed in Slovakia

Contents

About this book

AFTER THE FALL OF COMMUNISM we travelled Poland in a personal quest for the ghost of Chopin, whose music we both adore and play. We had already written our first Chopin study, *The Scottish Autumn of Frederick Chopin*, published by John Donald of Edinburgh, in 1994. Our researches led to the publication, in 1996, of our second Chopin book, *Chopin's Poland*, published by Peter Owen of London. At its launch at London's Sikorski Institute (at which the wine served was a Côtes de Nuits Villages, Domaine Chopin!) we displayed our personal photograph album of our travels, which was viewed with such interest and fascination that we asked our friend, artist and photographer Hanna Komarnicka, to recreate the album in her own, distinctive and highly creative manner. So, armed with a thick dossier of maps, details, books, pictures and our own humble book of "snaps", and a camera, the Komarnickis set off in search of Chopin's Poland...

Pamela & Iwo Załuski

WHEN OUR FRIENDS, the Załuskis, suggested an illustrated Chopin book we jumped at the chance to realise it and in this way we "discovered" Poland, following in the footsteps of the composer whom we have always loved and who is part of our heritage.

We were very lucky in having near perfect conditions during the trips that we made to Poland in order to photograph all the sites pictured in this book.

We consider that the four of us have contributed in different essential ways to the success and realisation of this book. Pamela was the researcher, Iwo – the writer, Hanna – the photographer, and Juliusz – the impresario who orchestrated the work and whose contacts and knowledge of the market led him to the final publisher...

We believe that between us we have a winning team of four professionals who together have produced a very attractive work, which is only the first of several that are already planned and in production.

Hanna & Juliusz Komarnicki

The Birth
of Chopin

IN 1782, IN THE VILLAGE OF DŁUGIE, in the Kujawy region of Poland, Antonina Krzyżanowska presented to her husband Jakub a little girl, who was baptised Justyna in the September of that year.

Five years later, a seventeenyear-old French youth, Nicolas Chopin, arrived in Warsaw to take up a job as cashier at Adam Weydlich's snuff factory. He was already familiar with things Polish as his father, François Chopin, had been employed as a wheelwright on the estate of the Polish magnate, Count Pac, at Marainville, near Nancy, the capital of Lorraine, known as "little Poland" because the Duke of Lorraine was the former King of Poland, Stanisław Leszczyński. Two years later the storming of the Bastille in Paris marked the beginning of the French Revolution, and Nicolas decided to stay in Poland.

...but finding ourselves in a foreign country where I can get on bit by bit, I would regret leaving here only to become a soldier, even in my own country.

NICOLAS CHOPIN to his family, 15th September 1790.

The bridge at **KIERNOZIA MANOR**

He had fallen in love with this vast, chaotic land, with its kaleidoscope of cultures, where Slavs, Germans, Jews and Balts writing in Roman, Gothic, Cyrillic and Hebrew scripts spoke a tower of Babel of languages and dialects, and worshipped in Roman Catholic, Russian Orthodox and Protestant churches and synagogues. Race, religion, fabulous wealth, and abysmal poverty all co-existed side by side in a state of tolerant apartheid.

Nicolas Chopin had adopted this fascinating and vibrant land as his own; yet it was in the throes of a spectacular decline that came to a head four years

40

The lake at **KIERNOZIA MANOR** ▶

THE MANOR AT KIERNOZIA, where Nicolas Chopin was tutor to the Łączyński family

after Nicolas' arrival in Warsaw. On the 3rd May 1791, King Stanisław August expressed the hopes and aspirations of the nation in signing a new constitution, inspired by the same liberal philosophies as had led to the American, and later, Napoleonic constitutions. This was unacceptable to the reactionary monarchies in Russia, Prussia and Austria, and over the next three years Poland was systematically partitioned by the three powers.

Nicolas Chopin's Poland ceased to exist, and he found himself living in the Prussian city of Warschau.

The view of **KIERNOZIA MANOR**

Economic and social collapse followed. Nicolas lost his job at the factory, and joined the insurrectionary forces under Tadeusz Kościuszko, French trained and charismatic freedom fighter who had risen to the rank of Colonel in the American War of Independence. Under his inspired, but ultimately unsuccessful leadership Nicolas saw action against the Russians. He befriended fellow fighter Maciej Łączyński, district governor at **KIERNOZIA**, to the west of Warsaw. In 1793 Nicolas and Maciej marched with Kościuszko to confront the Russians at Maciejowice.

THE CHURCH OF ST. ROCH AT BROCHÓW, where Nicolas and Justyna Chopin were married, and where Fryderyk Chopin was baptised ▶

was warmly received by Maciej's widow, Ewa, and her children at their manor, and at their house in nearby Czerniew. She offered Nicolas the post of tutor to her children, which he gratefully accepted.

On the 7th January 1807 at a reception in the Royal Castle in Warsaw, Napeoleon's eyes rested on the stunningly beautiful Maria Walewska. She was born Łączyńska, the fourth of five children, at Kiernozia, and had been tutored as a child by Nicolas Chopin. Her liaison with the Emperor is part of another story.

During this time Justyna Krzyżanowska left her home at Długie to help her cousin, Countess Ludwika Skarbek, at ŻELAZOWA WOLA in the Mazovian region, the family's only remaining property. Because of crippling Prussian taxes and a luxurious lifestyle the Skarbeks had lost nearly all their possessions. Count Kacper fled to Paris, leaving his wife to mind the estate, unassuming but idyllically situated on the banks of the RIVER UTRATA, and to bring up their three children, Fryderyk, Anna and Michał. Justyna's ambiguous brief – as a poor cousin – was to be a governess and live-in help about the house.

By 1802 the Łączyński children had grown up, and Nicolas, who had discovered that he had a talent for teaching and a way with youngsters, found a similar position with Countess Ludwika Skarbek of nearby Żelazowa Wola. He found the Skarbek children stimulating to teach, and they in turn responded to his warm and friendly methods. In later life Fryderyk Skarbek owed his brilliant academic career to his formative years with Nicolas Chopin's enlightened teaching.

> *Under this revered teacher... I received my first inclinations towards learning... which rested more on a general development of mental powers than on any training in particular subjects.*
>
> FRYDERYK SKARBEK "Memoirs" 1878.

The entrance of **THE CHURCH OF ST. ROCH AT BROCHÓW**

The battle was fierce. Maciej perished under the hooves of the Russian cavalry, Kościuszko was taken prisoner and Nicolas was wounded.

He returned to Warsaw to recover before setting off for KIERNOZIA, to inform Maciej's family of the circumstances of their friendship and of his death. He

The west wing of the former Skarbeks' **MANOR AT ŻELAZOWA WOLA,** the birthplace of Chopin

It was only a matter of time before the handsome Frenchman and the blonde young governess were seen to be spending much time in each others' company in this rural idyll on the banks of the River Utrata. Romance blossomed, and on the 28th June 1806 Nicolas and Justyna were married at the **CHURCH OF ST. ROCH** at **BROCHÓW**, near **ŻELAZOWA WOLA**. The wedding was celebrated to the familiar sounds of the *kujawiak* and the *oberek*, the dances with which the region is particularly associated. As a wedding present,

Countess Ludwika set aside the west wing of the manor for them.

In the autumn of that year Napoleon, having defeated the Prussians, marched into Prussian Poland to a delirious welcome, and proclaimed the Duchy of Warsaw, in effect a miniature new Poland, but in fact a French puppet state. Countess Skarbek moved her household to Warsaw, where, on the 6th April 1807, the Chopins' first child, Ludwika, named after the

The romantic atmosphere of **ŻELAZOWA WOLA** ▶

ŻELAZOWA WOLA, the recital room (formerly the living-room) where concerts are given every Sunday

Countess, was born. Napoleon's Warsaw fell short of expectations and became a stark and dangerous city, dedicated to servicing Napoleon's war machine, and the Skarbeks moved back to Żelazowa Wola.

On the 1st March 1810, according to the Chopin family, Justyna presented her husband with a baby boy in the alcove of their west wing of Żelazowa Wola, al-though according to the records at the Church of St. Roch the date was February 22nd. On the 23rd April the baby was baptised Fryderyk Franciszek at the Church of St. Roch. His godparents were Fryderyk and Anna Skarbek, although Franciszek Grembicki stood in for the absent Fryderyk Skarbek.

ŻELAZOWA WOLA, the restored alcove where Chopin was born ▶

Chopin's Warsaw

*P*ROFESSOR SAMUEL LINDE had been Rector of the Warsaw Lyceum since 1804. Fryderyk Skarbek had been a boarder there, and in the September of 1810 it would be Michał's turn. In that summer Professor Linde visited Żelazowa Wola to discuss his entry, and complained that he could not find a replacement for his sick French teacher. Nicolas Chopin's brief as tutor to the Skarbek children now effectively over, he accepted Linde's offer to fill the temporarily vacant post, and in October the Chopins moved to WARSAW.

The Lyceum was housed in the SAXON PALACE, off KRAKOWSKIE PRZEDMIEŚCIE, and an apartment on campus went with the post. Nicolas settled in to his new job and soon proved to be a brilliant and highly respected teacher, and his post was made permanent. Life in Napoleon's Duchy of Warsaw was tough and Nicolas

supplemented his meagre pay by taking in boarders. Justyna often took Ludka and Frycek – as baby Fryderyk was nicknamed – to the extensive SAXON GARDENS behind the Palace to gossip with the other Saxon Palace mothers.

All that remains to-day of THE SAXON PALACE, Chopin's first home in Warsaw – now the memorial to THE UNKNOWN SOLDIER

On the 9th July 1811 the Chopins' third child, Izabela, was born, and on January 1st of the following year Nicolas secured a part-time post teaching French at the School of Artillery in Długa Street. In the autumn of 1812 Napoleon launched his attack on Russia from Polish soil in Lithuania, and in Warsaw on the 20th November Justyna gave birth to Emilia. The child, nicknamed Emilka, was sickly, and it was feared she would not survive. The winter was harsh, and by the year's end survivors from Napoleon's disastrous campaign began to appear in Warsaw. Napoleon himself arrived, his Russian adventure over. He stayed briefly at the English Hotel, and

THE CASIMIR PALACE, now part of THE UNIVERSITY OF WARSAW, was the Chopins' second home in Warsaw. The Chopin apartment was on the second floor of the south wing ▶

It was a promising time for the Poles; there was a stability unknown for decades, and the economy was on the move. The arts flourished, especially music. Piano factories and music shops appeared everywhere. The Chopins had a fortepiano, and Justyna, herself an adequate pianist, was able to get hold of the latest compositions from Berlin, Vienna and St. Petersburg to play to the children. She taught Ludka the piano, and Ludka, in turn, passed on her lessons to Frycek.

In 1817 Grand Duke Constantine took over the Saxon Palace for military purposes, and the Lyceum was relocated at the **Casimir Palace** almost opposite. The Chopins' apartment was situated on the second floor of the south wing. Behind the Palace was **the Park**, where Ludka, Frycek, Izabela and Emilka played with the other children from the Palace. The following year **the University of Warsaw** was instituted in the main body of the Palace, creating a lively, academic atmosphere, which enhanced Warsaw's status as a growing and confident European city and centre of commerce and industry.

Frycek was now also being taught the piano by his mother, and he soon overtook his older sister. Nicolas and Justyna decided that Frycek should have formal piano lessons, and the elderly Bohemian, Woyciech Żywny, was engaged in 1816. Frycek and Żywny instantly took to each other, and the teacher-pupil partnership soon bore fruit. Frycek's technique went from strength to strength as Żywny introduced him to the contrapuntal complexities of Bach and the elegant grace of Mozart.

Frycek particularly loved the *Polonaises* and other dances of Ogiński which his mother brought back from Brzezina's music shop; shortly afterwards Frycek wrote several dances of his own in the same style. Some are now lost, but the *Polonaise in G minor*, his first published composition, survives, along with the *Polonaise in B flat*, both written when he was seven. Already by that time Frycek was aware of his unbreakable bond with the language of music.

The Park behind **the Casimir Palace** – formerly **the Botanical Gardens** – where Chopin played as a child with his sisters

stormed off westwards, and effectively out of the story of Poland. In his wake came the Russians, and Tsar Alexander's brother, Grand Duke Constantine, was installed as Military Governor of Warsaw at the **Belvedere Palace** in the south of the city.

Emilka survived, and life continued under the new régime. In 1815 the Congress of Vienna created the Kingdom of Poland with Tsar Alexander I as King.

The plaque commemorating Chopin on the outside of **the Casimir Palace** ▶

THE RADZIWIŁŁ PALACE, to-day the Presidential Palace, where the young Chopin gave his first concert in the French Theatre

I could express my feelings more easily if they could be put into notes of music, but as the very best concert would not cover my affection for you, dear papa, I must use the sim-ple words of my heart to lay before you my utmost gratitude and filial affection.

FRYDERYK CHOPIN's name day card to his father,
6th December 1818.

The Polonaise in G minor, Chopin's first published composition, written at the Casimir Palace when he was seven years old.
He dedicated it to Wiktoria Skarbek, a cousin of Countess Ludwika Skarbek

THE BENEVOLENT SOCIETY BUILDING in Krakowskie Przedmieście, where Chopin played for charity in front of the cream of Polish society ▶

THE BELVEDERE PALACE, where Chopin often came as a child to play for Grand Duke Constantine,
military Governor of Warsaw

Frycek began to play at concerts and soirées throughout Warsaw, and soon the word spread of a "Polish Mozart" in the city. He played at Countess Zamoyska's children's tea concerts at the **BŁĘKITNY PALACE** in Senatorska Street; he gave a charity performance of Gyrowetz's *Piano Concerto in E minor* at the French Theatre in the **RADZIWIŁŁ PALACE**. He played for charity at the **BENEVOLENT SOCIETY BUILDING** in Krakowskie Przedmieście, and at the residences of the highest Polish aristocracy.

Grand Duke Constantine sent a carriage to fetch Frycek to the **BELVEDERE PALACE**, initially to practise

French with his illegitimate son, Paul; but hearing Frycek improvising at the piano, the Duke was overwhelmed, and his visits became a regular occurrence; according to legend Frycek was the only person capable of soothing the Grand Duke out of his frequent temper tantrums, and the Duke's wife, the Princess of Łowicz, would send for Frycek on those occasions. When not playing for the Duke, who had one of Frycek's "military" improvisations orchestrated for marching band, he would be playing with Paul and Alexandrine de Moriolles, the daughter of Paul's tutor, the Comte de Moriolles. Frycek, Paul and "Moriolka" were the same age, so adventures and pranks in the

THE SMALL PALACE in the Łazienki Gardens ▶

THE CHOPIN MEMORIAL in the Łazienki Gardens

ŁAZIENKI GARDENS were the order of those days. Frycek's close friendship – and subsequent romance – with Moriolka continued until his final departure from Warsaw.

In 1822 Żywny declared that he could teach Frycek no more, although he remained a close friend of the family. Frycek dedicated his *Polonaise in A flat* to him as a name-day gift on April 23rd, 1821.

Twelve-year-old Chopin dedicated his *Polonaise in A flat* to his beloved teacher, Woyciech Żywny

THE EVANGELICAL CHURCH OF THE HOLY TRINITY, where Chopin played the *choralion* for Tsar Alexander I ▶

Fot. Stanisław Kolouszek

Commemorative plaque on the outside of **THE CASIMIR PALACE**

The plaque commemorating Woyciech Żywny, Chopin's first piano teacher, in **KRAKOWSKIE PRZEDMIEŚCIE** ▶

Architectural details in the **OLD TOWN**

Old sign in a courtyard in **KRAKOWSKIE PRZEDMIEŚCIE** ▶

The organ in **THE CHURCH OF THE VISITATION,** which Chopin regularly played during Mass

In the autumn of 1823 thirteen-year-old Frycek started at the Lyceum. He proved to be a bright and able pupil, and popular with his peers, especially his father's boarders. He had a talent for mimicry and drawing; his cartoons – including one of Professor Linde – were merciless, though the Professor was merciful enough to appreciate the humour. Frycek also enhanced his stories at the piano with music and dramatics; he was aided in this by Emilka, who was showing literary gifts with her writings and poetry; between them they formed "The Literary Society for Entertainment" for the delectation of their youthful audience. Among Frycek's closest friends were Dominik "Domuś" Dziewanowski and pianist Jan "Jaś" Białobłocki, both from estates in Mazovia.

The piano factories were booming, supplying the needs of the new Romanticism, as the younger generation of pianists looked for finer and more versatile instruments on which to display their virtuosity. Among their more fanciful creations were piano-harmonium hybrids, many replete with mechanical special effects. Like most boys in their mid-teens throughout history, Frycek was interested in new technology, and he spent many hours testing – and performing on – the *choralion*, the *eolimelodikon*, the *melodikordion*, the *melodipantaleon* and the *orchestron*, the creations of Hofman, Brunner and Buchholtz. He explored all their possibilities, and his fantastic improvisations – "orchestral" tone poems in their own right – showed that they were more than just extensions of the piano.

THE BELGIAN EMBASSY now occupies the site of the **MERCHANTS' HALL** in Senatorska Street

lost – to the Tsarina. Wishing to sample Warsaw's music manufacturing facilities, the Tsar attended a concert at the EVANGELICAL CHURCH OF THE HOLY TRINITY, off Królewska Street, at which Frycek gave an improvisation on the *choralion*. The delighted Tsar presented him, and the manufacturer, Brunner, each with a diamond ring. That summer Frycek's Op. 1, the *Rondo in C minor*, dedicated to the second Mme Linde, was published.

The Tsar died later that year, and was succeeded by his younger brother, Nicholas I.

Frycek played the organ at the CHURCH OF THE VISITATION next to the CASIMIR PALACE, whenever the boys of the Lyceum attended Mass there. His knack of leading from the hymns and responses into his improvisations was legendary, and he sometimes became so carried away that he had to be restrained to enable the service to continue.

> *I am appointed organist to the Lyceum... the most important person in the whole Lyceum after his reverence the priest. Every Sunday I play the organ for the* Wizytki *and the others sing.*
>
> FRYDERYK CHOPIN to JAN BIAŁOBŁOCKI,
> November 1825.

In the spring of 1825 Tsar Alexander came to Warsaw to open the Seym, and to see how his western Kingdom was faring. During a grand tour redolent with benevolence, he came to the Lyceum, and called on Nicolas' class – Frycek was placed in it for the occasion. He formally presented a set of dances – now

In the autumn of 1826 Frycek enrolled at the Main School of Music, which later became the Warsaw Music Conservatory, which was a department of the University. The Rector, opera composer Józef Elsner, who lived at Krakowskie Przedmieście No. 56 with his wife and family, had already been preparing Frycek unofficially by bridging the gap left by Żywny's resignation. The course involved intensive cramming of the rules of form, harmony, counterpoint and orchestration, as well as pianism. Frycek coped well with the latter, but had great difficulties with orchestration and his

THE KRASIŃSKI PALACE in Krakowskie Przedmieście, to which the Chopin family moved in 1827 ▶

attempts at fugue have not found their way into the repertoire. He dedicated his first *Piano Sonata in C minor, Op. 4*, to Elsner – a dedication that he later withdrew as he did not deem it good enough.

Frycek took to the student life well. He had many friends, including Wilhelm "Wiluś" Kolberg, who lived downstairs, pianists Julian Fontana and Tytus Woyciechowski, who had an estate at Poturzyn, beyond Zamość, and Jan Matuszyński. He frequent-

Vivace

Chopin dedicated his *Rondo à la Mazur, Op. 5* to his boyhood sweetheart, Countess Alexandrine de Moriolles, known as "Moriolka"

ly went with them to the opera in Krasiński Square, or set the world to rights in Warsaw's cafés; the **DZIURKA** and the **HONORATKA** in Miodowa Street, and the two on either side of the **POST OFFICE** in Kozia Street, the **BAROKA** and **MRS BRZE-ZIŃSKA'S**.

Frycek's girlfriend during his teenage years was Alexandrine "Moriolka" de Moriolles, as we have mentioned before. One of their preferred meeting places was the park behind the University, which had now become the **BOTANICAL GARDENS**. Frycek dedicated

Early evening in **WARSAW'S OLD MARKET SQUARE**

his *Rondo à la Mazur, Op. 5* to her.

If you knew what changes there are in our Botanical Gardens, they have put such flower beds, paths, plantations, shrubs and so on, that it's a pleasure to go in, especially as we have a key.

FRYDERYK CHOPIN to JAN BIAŁOBŁOCKI, June 1826.

On the 10th April 1827 Emilka, aged fourteen, died of tuberculosis and was buried in the **POWĄZKI CEMETERY**. The Chopin family were devastated, and shortly afterwards they moved to a much larger apartment on the second floor of the

KRASIŃSKI PALACE, where Frycek wrote his *Variations on Mozart's La ci darem la mano for Piano and Orchestra, Op. 2* – his first attempt at scoring for orchestra.

> *There's a room upstairs which is to be at my service; steps have been made to it from the wardrobe room. I am to have an old piano there, and it is to be my den.*
>
> FRYDERYK CHOPIN to TYTUS WOYCIECHOWSKI,
> 27th December 1828.

In early 1828 both Countess Ludwika Skarbek and Frycek's friend Jaś Białobłocki died of tuberculosis. These deaths reinforced Frycek's own sense of mortality; he had also been showing symptoms of the disease, which, even though apparently under control, was a constant worry.

> *Everybody's falling ill, and I too... This scribbling comes out of a head that's tied up in a nightcap because it has been aching for the last four days. They have put leeches on my throat because the glands have swelled.*
>
> FRYDERYK CHOPIN to JAN BIAŁOBŁOCKI,
> 12th February 1826.

Karol Soliwa was the Conservatory's leading teacher of singing, and among his star students was the beautiful and talented Konstancja Gładkowska. Frycek had often accompanied her during practices, but it was during a concert arranged by Soliwa in early 1829 that he fell hopelessly in love with her. Being shy, he kept this love to himself, and confided only to Tytus Woyciechowski and Jan Matuszyński that he had found his "ideal". No exhortations to declare himself bore any fruit; Frycek seemed determined to keep her on a pedestal – an impossible, unattainable dream.

Frycek suffered his way through the year, and in July he graduated from the Conservatory with Elsner's typically terse report: "Szopen Friderik (special ability, musical genius, etc)". Frycek applied to the Ministry of Public Instruction for a grant to continue his studies in Vienna. His application was turned down on the documented grounds that "public funds should not be wasted for the encouragement of this type of artist". This was a blow for Frycek, already depressed about the constant threat of tuberculosis, his secret passion for Konstancja and a crisis of confidence.

He went to Vienna anyway, and on his return his melancholy took hold once more. He gave a concert at the "old" MERCHANTS' HALL in Miodowa Street (the "new" Merchants' Hall was in Senatorska Street) and returned to composition, expressing his love for Konstancja with an Adagio; this turned into the slow movement of his *Piano Concerto in F minor*. The Concerto was premiered with a small ensemble on the 3rd March 1830 in the Chopins' apartment in the KRASIŃSKI PALACE to a very select gathering musicians and journalists. After a very favourable reaction this was followed by a full concert performance at the National Theatre in Krasiński Square on March 17th. But even before this performance Frycek was already writing the slow movement of his second *Concerto in E minor*, again a poem of love to his beloved Konstancja. The concerto was premiered, again at the National Theatre, on October 11th.

> *You can't imagine what misery are the last three days before a concert.*
>
> FRYDERYK CHOPIN to TYTUS WOYCIECHOWSKI,
> 27th March 1830.

By the time Frycek left Warsaw, and his homeland, for the last time in 1830, he had written all his works for piano and orchestra.

42

The plaque outside **THE KRASIŃSKI PALACE** commemorating Chopin's last address in Poland ▶

Holidays in Mazovia

CHAPTER

*M*AZOVIA, THE AGRARIAN LANDS astride the RIVER VISTULA to the north-west of Warsaw, is the home of the mazurka, which, along with the polonaise, represents the soul of Polish dance more than any other. During his several visits to the region as a teenager Frycek picked up the subtle nuances of this music to use in his own *Mazurkas*: the "bagpipe" drone, the use of dissonance and ambiguous sense of key, and modal tonalities. Dance bands, which included bagpipes, hurdy-gurdy hybrids and other fanciful devices as well as violins, clarinet and double bass were numerous, and the Jewish ones were considered to be the best.

Frycek's closest friend during his first year at the Lyceum was Domuś Dziewanowski, and in July 1824 he went to spend the summer holidays at Domuś' family's estate in SZAFARNIA. The two boys spent their time exploring the countryside, playing on the banks of the lake in the grounds of the estate, and being taken on outings by Domuś' fun-loving Aunt Ludwika.

On the banks of THE RIVER VISTULA

You're not the only one who can ride; I can as well, but don't ask how well, but I can, enough to let the horse go slowly wherever it wants to, while I sit on it, terrified, like a monkey on a bear.

FRYDERYK CHOPIN to WILHELM KOLBERG, August 1824.

Frycek was fascinated with the quirks of country life, and, encouraged by Domuś, he edited his own whimsical local paper based on the format of "The Warsaw Courier", which he then sent home as a newsheet. Four "editions" of "The Szafarnia Courier" were "published", and throw considerable light on life in Mazovia at the time from the point of view of a teenaged city-dweller with a sense of humour. As the intrepid

THE MANOR AT SZAFARNIA, the home of Chopin's school friend, Dominik Dziewanowski, where Chopin spent the summer holidays of 1824 and 1825. To-day it is the venue of Chopin concerts and festivals ▶

THE MANOR AT SOKOŁOWO, the home of Chopin's ill-fated school friend, Jan Białobłocki, whom Chopin visited in 1824 and 1825. The Manor is one of the few original Chopin sites remaining in Poland

reporter, "Mr Pichon" (an anagram of Chopin), Frycek reported a harvest festival at **OBROWO**, a wedding at **BOCHENIEC**, how in **NIESZAWA** "Mr Pichon" had to bribe a peasant girl sitting on a fence with *3 groszy* to repeat her rendition, in an incomprehensible local accent, of a local folk song that had caught his imagination, and the unsuccessful attempts at peaceful co-existence by a turkey and a kite at **SOKOŁOWO**.

"The Szafarnia Courier" had two sections; "Home News" reported events in Szafarnia itself.

On August 15ᵗʰ there was a musical gathering at Szafarnia of a score or so of miscellaneous persons. Mr Pichon figured in the programme with a piano concerto by Kalkbrenner. This did not have as much effect on the miscellaneous persons as the żydek *performed by the same Mr Pichon.*

"Szafarnia Courier" Issue No. 2, 19ᵗʰ August 1824.

"Foreign News" dealt with observations picked up during trips further afield. One of these was an

A view of **GOLUB-DOBRZYŃ**. In Chopin's day the frontier with Prussia was the River Drwęca which runs through the town ▶

The ancient **CASTLE IN GOLUB-DOBRZYŃ**, where Chopin listened to street musicians in the courtyard

excursion to GOLUB, whose enormous market was covered by "Mr. Pichon... this intrepid traveller". In the corner of the market square there was a PROTESTANT CHURCH which Frycek and his friends visited. It was being renovated. Frycek climbed into the pulpit and delivered a sermon, mimicking the German vicar who had trouble with pronouncing Polish. The sermon was met with laughter from both his friends and the workmen.

Chopin's *Mazurka in B flat* of 1825 was published without an opus number.
It uses the Lydian mode, with the sharpened 4th, a common device in Mazovia and Kujawy

The courtyard of **THE PROTESTANT CHURCH IN GOLUB-DOBRZYŃ**, where Chopin amused the workmen doing restorations, and his friends, by mimicking the Pastor from the pulpit ▶

ed the magnificent mediaeval **CASTLE**, perched spectacularly on its hill. It was originally built by the Teutonic Knights and extensively restored in the seventeenth century. The courtyard was full of merchants, beggars, peasants, tourists and street entertainers. Frycek was amused by a musician churning out the staierek, or German waltz, on his hurdy-gurdy, and expressed his disdain in verse.

> *Miss Ludwika gave half-zloty*
> *To listen to a Prussian waltz,*
> *If it hadn't been for Miss Ludwika*
> *For such songs there'd be no calls.*

During this holiday Frycek went to the mediaeval Prussian city of Thorn, as **TORUŃ** was known then. He stayed at the **FENGER PALACE** in Mostowa Street; wealthy banker Jakub Fenger was Countess Ludwika Skarbek's father. He was singularly impressed with the magnificent buildings, and drank in the history; he described seeing the **HOUSE** – and the very room – where **COPERNICUS** was born, the **CHURCHES OF ST. JOHN**, of **THE BLESSED VIRGIN** and of **ST. JACOB**, the **TOWN HALL**, and the **CROOKED TOWER**. But what he liked most of all were the gingerbread cakes – in Polish called *pierniki* – local specialities which came in every shape from a biscuit to a sculpted coach and horses. He sent one such cake home for Emilka.

> *But never mind Copernicus; let us start*
> *with the Toruń cakes... I just want to say*
> *that it's these* pierniki *that impressed me*
> *the most. It's true that I have seen all the*
> *fortifications... the famous contraption for*
> *shifting sand... all the Gothic churches go-*
> *ing back to the Teutonic Knights... the lean-*
> *ing tower, the famous town hall... None of*
> *this beats the* pierniki *– oh! the* pierniki*...*
> FRYDERYK CHOPIN to JAN MATUSZYŃSKI, August 1825.

THE CHURCH OF ST. JOHN, TORUŃ

Frycek was again invited to **SZAFARNIA** for the holidays the following year. Once more Frycek and Domuś went with Aunt Ludwika to **GOLUB**, but this time they crossed the bridge over the little **RIVER DRWĘCA** into Prussia to visit the town of **DOBRZYŃ** on the other side. They visit-

One Sunday Frycek went to spend the day with another school friend, Jaś Białobłocki. Jaś, seriously ill

53

A detail of one of **THE GRANARIES IN TORUŃ**

Toruń's famous **CROOKED TOWER** ▶

A detail from the entrance to **THE CHURCH OF ST. JOHN IN TORUŃ**

with tuberculosis, lived in **SOKOŁOWO** at the Manor of his stepfather, Antoni Wybraniecki. Both were pianists, and Mr Wybraniecki was the proud owner of a pantaleon, and the two boys spent the day experimenting on it before going to the orchard to eat apples. Jaś was now so ill that there was no chance of his returning to school in the autumn.

The central section of Chopin's *Mazurka in A flat, Op. 7 No. 4,* written in Mazovia, features the distinctive bagpipe drone in the bass

The tower of **THE TORUŃ TOWN HALL** ▶

SANNIKI MANOR, where Chopin stayed with his school friend, Konstanty Pruszak, in the summer of 1828

I at once remembered Sokołowo, that Sunday, the pantaleons, the apples, and other joyful past moments.

FRYDERYK CHOPIN TO JAN BIAŁOBŁOCKI,
8th September 1825.

On his return from Szafarnia in the autumn of 1825, Frycek kept in touch with the now severely crippled Jaś, sent music from Mr Brzezina's shop for him to play, or some of his own "scribblings", and did what he could to cheer him up. Jaś' death, three years later, affected Frycek deeply.

In 1828 Frycek visited another part of Mazovia, when he spent the summer holidays at SANNIKI, the country home of his school friend Kostuś Pruszak. The Pruszaks also had a Warsaw house in Marszałkowska Street, where amateur dramatics, in which Frycek took enthusiastic part, were the order of the day. That summer Sanniki was full of young people; there were open air charades and plays alternating with local dances at which the swirl of the distinctive local costumes accompanied the sounds of the mazurka, the *kujawiak* and the *oberek*, as the youngsters danced and loved into the night, and even the shy Frycek became embroiled in a scandal – later proved unfounded – involving a young governess.

The entrance of **THE CHURCH OF THE HOLY TRINITY AT SANNIKI** ▶

A Journey to
the Silesian Waters

CHAPTER 4

TUBERCULOSIS WAS ONE OF THE BANES of nineteenth century Warsaw, and it claimed many lives prematurely. Of the Chopin children, Emilka and Frycek both showed symptoms of this frightening wasting disease. Taking the waters was considered beneficial in some cases, and Frycek's school friend, Jaś Białobłocki, spoke of his visit to the spa at Bischoffswerter, in eastern Prussia. In 1826 Rector of the Music Conservatory Józef Elsner, born and bred in Silesia, recommended the waters at Reinertz – now called Duszniki-Zdrój – a pretty spa town in the Sudeten Mountains to the south of the Silesian capital of Breslau – as **WROCŁAW** was known then.

The Chopins and the Skarbeks decided to make up a party to spend the summer holidays of 1826 taking the Silesian waters. Because of various commitments they travelled in three separate groups; Ludka Chopin, a devotee of child psychology and a budding writer of moral tales for children, like her literary heroine, Klementyna Tańska, travelled with Frycek's godfather, Fryderyk Skarbek, his wife Prakseda, and their seven-year-old son, Józio. Ludka later wrote and published a moral tale entitled "Józio's Journey from Warsaw to the Silesian Spas, as written by himself", which documented their trip in some detail. Countess Ludwika Skarbek, also a tuberculosis sufferer, and the now very frail Emilka, followed a few days later.

Frycek had to wait till his final school examinations were over. Before his departure he and his school friend, Wiluś Kolberg, celebrated the end of Frycek's schooling at the opera, where they saw Rossini's *The Thieving Magpie*. It was a memorable performance, and afterwards Frycek, apprehensive about the trip and its significance, wrote a Polonaise as an adieu to Wiluś; the Trio of the *Polonaise in B flat minor* is a reworking of a Gianetto aria from *The Thieving Magpie*.

A detail of **THE TOWN HALL IN WROCŁAW** ▶

THE MARKET SQUARE IN WROCŁAW

The Trio from the *Polonaise in B flat minor* is based on an aria from Rossini's *The Thieving Magpie*

On July 28th Frycek and his mother set off from the Post Office in Kozia Street by stage-coach; Izabela and her father stayed at home. They passed through **BŁONIE**, **SOCHACZEW**, which Frycek visited several times, and **ŁOWICZ**, where they probably stayed at the Post Hotel in Wjazdowa Street. It was to Łowicz that the body of Polish hero Józef Poniatowski was brought to lie in state at the Collegiate Church after his death at the

The baroque monument in **THE MARKET SQUARE, DUSZNIKI** ▶

THE TOWN HALL in the Market Square, **DUSZNIKI**

Battle of the Five Nations in 1813. They continued through KUTNO, KŁODAWA, KOŁO, TUREK and KALISZ, where Frycek always stayed with his friend Dr Adam Helbich. Just beyond Kalisz was the Prussian border at Biskupice, where the new paved road, built by Alexander I, came to an end and the rutted Prussian dirt track continued to OSTRÓW. On this occasion Frycek and his mother did not call at nearby STRZYŻEW, where Frycek's godmother and Countess Skarbek's daughter, Anna, lived with her husband, Stefan Wiesiołowski, and her young children, Ludwika and Roman. The other parties stopped there on the way to call on family and to visit the grave of Count Kacper Skarbek at the church in nearby KOTŁÓW. The road

continued through MIĘDZYBÓRZ, OLEŚNICA, dominated by its fourteenth-century Castle, and historic WROCŁAW. Here, in 1109, Bolesław Krzywousty (the Wrymouth) defeated the Emperor Henry V and the Duke of Bohemia at the bloody battle of Psie Pole (literally "Dog's Field") just outside the city. The victory forced the Germans to renounce all claims to that Polish territory. History had passed, and Wrocław was again a German city. The post road led straight through the historic battlefield.

This was the first of Frycek's several visits to Wrocław. The magnificent Market Square's hostelries featured the traditional "golden" prefix. The Skarbeks and the

A detail of the Chopin memorial, **DUSZNIKI-ZDRÓJ** ▶

THE MANOR IN DUSZNIKI-ZDRÓJ, where Chopin gave two concerts in August 1826. To-day it is the Concert Hall and venue of the annual Duszniki Chopin Festival

Chopin girls stayed at the "Golden Tree", opposite the TOWN HALL, where they had a first class view of its astronomical clock.

We are staying in the Market Square itself, and the inn has a golden tree as its sign. Opposite is the Town Hall, old and dirty, and yet they say it's very beautiful. Beneath my window there are stalls with merchants who have come to the market.

"Józio's Journey..." by LUDWIKA CHOPIN, Warsaw 1830.

Frycek and his mother stayed at the "Golden Goose" in Oławska Street. Elsner had given Frycek three letters of introduction to musical friends of his, but time was short, and Frycek could only call on one of them.

After Wrocław came NIEMCZA, ZĄBKOWICE ŚLĄSKIE, BARDO, where the road climbed into the mountains, and KŁODZKO; Frycek and his mother arrived at DUSZNIKI on August 3rd, after a week on the road. The town consisted of Duszniki itself and, two kilometres away, DUSZNIKI-ZDRÓJ the spa complex. The Skarbek contingent, with Ludka, stayed at the house of Burgermeister

The little bridge over **THE RIVER BYSTRZYCA IN DUSZNIKI-ZDRÓJ** ▶

THE HERMITAGE, the decorative gate with the Chopin monogram

to their well for the first intake of water. Frycek's well was the Lau-Brunn, an elevated podium with safety railings round a deep hole in the ground where the bubbling, steaming water could be seen several feet down. Guests were not allowed to help themselves, for fear of dizziness – or at worst asphixiation – from the gaseous waters exuding carbon dioxide in unsafe quantities. Everyone was served by attendant girls who scooped the water in a jug at the end of a pole, and handed out ginger biscuits to neutralise the unpleasant taste of the water. The rest of the morning was spent walking and socialising in the grounds to the accompaniment of the spa wind band, an execrable outfit led by a thin bassoonist with a snuff-stained, bespectacled nose.

> *It was a lovely day, which is why everyone was strolling in the gardens full of lovely flowers, roses and mallows. I enjoyed the music, although Papa was cross because they played out of tune.*
>
> "Józio's Journey..." by LUDWIKA CHOPIN,
> Warsaw 1830.

It was normal to wear masks, to give the morning a carnival atmosphere. At noon everyone went to their lodgings for lunch, after which the second water intake took place. The afternoon was spent again promenading – in a change of costume – to the sound of the wind band. After supper most guests went to bed in anticipation of rising early, or visited each other to socialise. For the more adventurous, there were many delightful walks in the green, forested hills surrounding the town, including the road to the village of **PODGÓRZE**. The banks of the **RIVER BYSTRZYCA** was also a favourite place to walk and admire its many little tributaries, especially the **BIAŁY POTOK**, tumbling in flower-bedecked waterfalls towards the valley. Frycek complained that he was forbidden to climb the hill of **ZŁOTA SZTOLNIA** as the air was not considered beneficial in his case.

August Heine, at the spa, while Frycek, Emilka and their mother lodged at Burgel's Hof, a guest house close by. The whole spa was criss-crossed with leafy walkways lined with flowerbeds, which connected the residences with the well-houses. The guests were mostly Germans, Poles and Czechs – the Bohemian border was only a few kilometres away.

The régime was the same for everyone. The day began at six in the morning when everyone reported

The gate of **THE HERMITAGE AT DUSZNIKI-ZDRÓJ** with the Fryderyk Chopin Monogram (FC) ▶

I have already been up the hill known as Einsideley [sic] because of the hermit there. Having climbed to the top of this hill, one of the highest in Reynertz [sic], up well over a hundred steep steps of cut stone going up in a straight line, one gets to the hermit, and from there there is a splendid view of the whole of Reynertz.

FRYDERYK CHOPIN to WILHELM KOLBERG,
18th August 1826.

Duszniki Town was a favoured social haunt, notably "U Niedźwiedzia" ("The Bear Inn") in the Market Square. This hostelry was patronised by all the cream of Polish and Prussian society, and its most famous lodger was King Jan Kazimierz, who spent a night there in 1669. Industry co-existed dubiously side by side with nature at Duszniki. The town boasted a **PAPER MILL** on the banks of the river, where the manager took guests on guided tours, and in the Strążyska Valley Mendelssohn's (an uncle of the composer) iron foundry spewed black smoke over the hills.

Frycek climbed the 150 steps up the **EINSIEDELEI HILL** to the **HERMITAGE**, which was occupied by a solitary Catholic priest, who was supported by the people of Duszniki. It consisted of one room, a chapel and a small vegetable garden. According to legend, in 1698 the children of Duszniki climbed the hill, knelt and prayed for deliverance from a plague that was ravaging the region. Their prayers were answered, Duszniki was spared, and the people built the Hermitage and installed a priest in thanks for their deliverance. The arrangement was still maintained in Chopin's day.

THE HERMITAGE, which to-day is the Museum
of the Chopin Festival

The attendant at Lau-Brunn was a Czech girl called Libusza, whose father worked at the foundry. Her mother had died several years previously, and Libusza also acted as housewife and mother to her four younger siblings. She was popular with everyone because of her charming manner and cheery smile; her charms were not lost on sixteen-year-old Frycek, who called on her at home several times.

A legend has grown around Frycek's friendship with Libusza, based on true events, but whose details have not been fully substantiated.

Over to the left was a wall lined with bushes and a row of wooden crosses. The hermit said they were the graves of his predecessors, and that his own cross would be there one day.

"Józio's Journey..." by LUDWIKA CHOPIN,
Warsaw 1830.

One day there was an accident at the foundry, Libusza's father was crushed to death by a roller, and the children were all orphaned. Frycek's condolences were particularly heartfelt; encouraged by his mother, he took steps to arrange a concert for the orphans' benefit. The local council was very co-operative, and the small Manor in the centre of the spa, which had

The oldest surviving **PAPER MILL** in Poland, which Chopin visited

a passable piano, was chosen as the venue. The concert took place on about August 11th (the exact date is not known). It was such a resounding success, and raised a goodly sum, that a repeat performance was arranged for August 16th. The children's plight was thus highlighted, Libusza went to stay with an aunt in Prague, while the other children were taken into care by the council. Frycek's philanthropy was reported in the Warsaw press, and Żywny wrote to Frycek, congratulating him on his generosity of spirit.

On September 11th Frycek and his mother set off for home, several days after the rest of the party. The time had come for Frycek to think about his impending first term at the Warsaw Conservatory of Music under Józef Elsner, who would be waiting to hear all about Frycek's Silesian experience.

Towards the Baltic Sea

AFTER THE TRAGIC DEATH from tuberculosis of Emilka Chopin in the spring of 1827, her godfather, Count Ksawery Zboiński, a relative of the Dziewanowskis of SZAFARNIA, wanted to do something positive for Frycek, for whom the tragedy carried the added implication of his own vulnerability; he proposed a trip to family estates in east Prussia and Danzig, as Gdańsk was then called, in the summer. A further opportunity arose when wealthy landowner, violinist, composer and patron of music Count Antoni Sierakowski was planning his summer guest list to his estate at Waplewo, near Malbork in east Prussia, and also invited Frycek, whose musicianship he admired enormously. With the cheering prospect of a musical summer, and a chance to put the tragedy behind him, Frycek gladly accepted the invitation. Also invited was Count Ignacy Dembowski, who lived in Warsaw, and undertook to chaperone Frycek during the trip.

The Chopins had just moved to their new apartment at the Krasiński Palace, opposite the University and the Lyceum. At the end of July, Frycek had finished his first year at the Conservatory, and Elsner's typically terse end-of-year report read "special ability". Count Dembowski arrived to pick Frycek up to take him to Count Ksawery's Mazovian estate at KOWALEWO for a

short stay with the Count, his wife and three little daughters – including two-year-old Kamilka, or "Kagila" as she called herself, who fell madly in love with Frycek. The stay was pleasant, and Frycek even composed a waltz, which is now lost.

> *We're just starting; it's eight in the morning... the air is fine, the sun is shining beautifully, the birds are twittering; there isn't a brook, or it would murmur, but there is a pond, and the frogs are in fine voice. But the very best of all is a blackbird singing about all manner of adventures under our windows.*
>
> FRYDERYK CHOPIN to his parents,
> July 1827.

At eight o'clock on the morning of the last Friday in July, the carriage of the Zboiński party set off for east Prussia. First stop was the ancient city of PŁOCK on the RIVER VISTULA. Count Ksawery was now a senator at the Seym, but had latterly been Superintendent of Płock Castle, which he wanted to show to Frycek. The historic centre of the city, with its still surviving mediaeval walls and towers, was known as "Little Cracow". The next day the party continued to ROŚCISZEWO, and stayed with Rościszewski family. The following day

PŁOCK, Cathedral interior

THE LAKE OF KIKÓŁ at dusk ▶

THE PALACE AT KIKÓŁ, home of Count Józef Zboiński, where Chopin is reputed to have played the piano

being a Sunday, the whole party attended mass in the village church before continuing to KIKÓŁ, and the home of Count Józef Zboiński, another member of that large family. Count Józef lived in magnificent splendour at the sumptuous Kikół Palace, situated on a hill overlooking a lake. In the Knight's Hall there was a fortepiano, which Frycek is reputed to have played.

The party continued to the bridge at LUBICZ, on the RIVER DRWĘCA, which was the Prussian border; there they turned north, to bypass TORUŃ, and make for TURZNO, where they stayed for a couple of days with yet more relatives, the Gajewskis, at their manor, which was in effect two completely different manors, side by side. The next port of call was another Zboiński residence, that of Count Karol, at KOZŁOWO. This estate was situated on the banks of the RIVER WDA, which joined the River Vistula at Świecie, then called Schwetz, a few kilometres

downstream. Again the party stayed for a few days, after which Count Józef joined the party for the last lap of the trip, and on August 9th, after nearly a fortnight, the Zboiński carriage drove through the Golden Gate of the historic city of GDAŃSK. The party put up at the prestigious "Drei Mohren" hotel, where they were met by Count Antoni Sierakowski, who had come over from Waplewo to meet them and play the host and guide.

After five days Count Antoni invited the party to spend a week at his estate at WAPLEWO. For Frycek it was a stimulating week making and talking music with one of east Prussia's most talented and enthusiastic patrons of music. Frycek spent a further five days in GDAŃSK before returning home to Warsaw. The experience had done him some good, but his mother never recovered from Emilka's death, and was still unconsolable. She wore black for the rest of her life.

THE MANOR AT TURZNO, where Chopin and the Zboińskis stayed with the Gajewski family ▶

Wielkopolska

FRYCEK **L**OVED **T**RAVELLING, and every summer he accepted invitations from his many friends, relatives and admirers to their country residences, notably in Wielkopolska, which broadly covers western Poland. Before starting at the Lyceum, Frycek spent the summer holidays in Żelazowa Wola with his parents and sisters. Since their departure the manor had burnt down and been rebuilt. Countess Ludwika Skarbek was now on her own, as her children had left home: Frycek's godfather Fryderyk to pursue a brilliant academic career at the University, and his godmother Anna to marry Stefan Wiesiołowski and set up home in Strzyżew, near Kalisz at the Prussian border.

1823 was a lovely summer, and Frycek spent a few days back at Żelazowa Wola. Friends and family called often, and for Frycek's benefit the piano was taken out into the garden.

Everyone spread themselves out throughout the orchard, and even people from the neighbouring villages came running to the gates to listen to the visitor from Warsaw.

Recollections of A<small>NTONI</small> K<small>RYSIAK</small> to M<small>ILY</small> B<small>ALAKIREV</small>, 1890.

Piano at **ANTONIN** on which concerts are regularly given

The sounds of the piano attracted the villagers, including thirteen-year-old Antoni Krysiak, who congregated at the gates to listen, spellbound, to the sounds of the thirteen-year-old boy from Warsaw improvising during the balmy evenings.

In 1827 Frycek's younger sister, Emilka, died of tuberculosis. After his return from Gdańsk and Waplewo, Frycek, who still had not got over her death, went to stay with the Wiesiołowskis in **STRZYŻEW** for a few days. He visited them every time he was in the region, and on those occasions he

THE **H**UNTING **L**ODGE **A**T **A**NTONIN where Chopin was a guest of Prince Antoni Radziwiłł ▶

and married Princess Ludwika of Prussia. He carved out a career as a Prussian statesman and a patron of music. After the Congress of Vienna, King Friedrich Wilhelm III appointed him Governor of the Duchy of Posen, as Poznań was then called. In 1826 his remarkable, octagonal, four-winged timber **HUNTING LODGE** in the forests to the south of Poznań, named **ANTONIN** after himself, was completed. It was there that the Prince liked to relax with his family, to arrange hunting parties and to make music. He was a highly respected composer, an accomplished cellist, and had a fine tenor voice.

Frycek's first visit to Antonin was on his return from Duszniki in September 1826, when he called on the Prince. He met Princess Ludwika and their two beautiful daughters, Wanda and Eliza; the former a pianist, and the latter an artist, whose famous sketch of Frycek at the piano, was drawn on this occasion.

Frycek also enjoyed the warm hospitality of the Radziwiłł household at the Prince's official residence in **POZNAŃ**, which he visited in the autumn of 1828 during a trip to Berlin. Warsaw University Professor Feliks Jarocki had been invited to an international congress of Naturalists in the Prussian capital, and offered to take Frycek with him for the experience. Frycek's interest in natural science was minimal, and he was mildly bored, but concerts and the opera gave him some relief. At one reception he caught a glimpse of Felix Mendelssohn, the young German pianist with a growing reputation. Their eyes met momentarily, but Frycek was too shy to approach him, and the two giants of Romantic pianism failed to meet by a whisker of reticence.

On the way back from Berlin the stage-coach passed through **SULECHÓW**, or Zullechau, as the town was then called. Many years later Fryderyk's sister, Izabela, reported that the passengers stopped at the Post Stage in the Market Square. As there were

The interior chimney at **ANTONIN**

also sometimes stayed with Prince Radziwiłł at nearby **ANTONIN**. The Prince heard Frycek play at the fashionable Warsaw salon of Princess Czetwertyńska in 1825, and extended an open invitation to Antonin.

Prince Antoni Radziwiłł was born in Vilnius in 1775 into one of Lithuania's most illustrious families. He studied singing and the cello in Berlin, where he met

In the park of **ANTONIN** ▶

The lake at **ANTONIN**

no fresh horses available, the driver announced a delay. The apologetic postmaster invited the coach party to refreshments at his house in nearby Tuchmacher Street. Seated in the lounge, Frycek saw a piano in the next room. He walked over to it and was soon improvising. Noticing an elderly German standing in the doorway, listening, Frycek decided to give him a taste of some Polish folk music, and launched into a grand medley of Polish airs which wafted all the way down the street.

Young man, I'd have given ten years of my life to be able to play like you. If Mozart had heard you he'd have shaken your hand and cried "Bravo!"

IZABELA BARCIŃSKA'S, née Chopin, account of the recollections of CANTOR KAHLER, music teacher of Sulechów, on hearing Chopin playing at the Postmaster's house.

Soon the house was beset by travellers and locals, all crowding round to listen. The delighted postmaster, his

90

The tower of **THE TOWN HALL, SULECHÓW** ▶

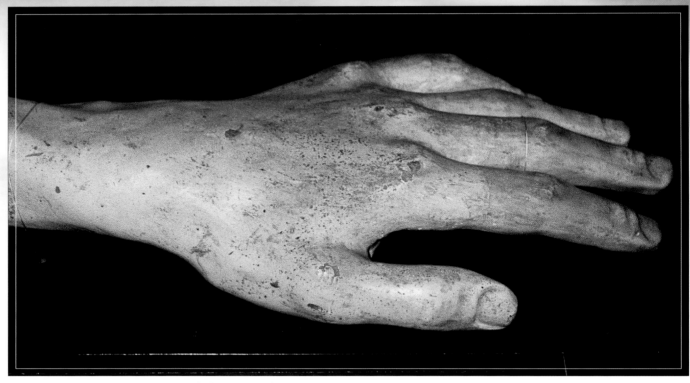

Cast of Chopin's hand at **THE POZNAŃ MUSEUM OF MUSICAL INSTRUMENTS**

wife and two pretty daughters served cakes and and sweets, and a party atmosphere ensued. When the driver eventually interrupted to say that fresh horses had been harnessed and the coach was all set to go, he was waved impatiently away. By then Frycek was feeling very tired, but still his audience wanted to hear more. When eventually he climbed, ex-

hausted, into the coach, more sweets and cakes were pressed into his pockets for the next stage to **POZNAŃ**. After the Sulechów experience Frycek began to formulate in his mind a composition for piano and orchestra based on Polish folk songs. The idea eventually took shape as the *Grand Fantasy on Polish Airs, Op. 13*.

The folk melody, *Laura and Filon*, which Chopin used in his *Grand Fantasy on Polish Airs, Op. 13*.
The arrangement by Iwo Załuski

The fountain in **THE OLD TOWN SQUARE IN POZNAŃ** ▶

comed by the Prince, who immediately arranged a concert at the Residence to an invited gathering of **POZNAŃ** society. The Prince gave musical soirées, and maintained a regular string quartet, in which he himself played the cello.

The following year, Frycek, after his return from Vienna, again spent some golden autumn days with the Radziwiłł family, at **ANTONIN**. Prince Radziwiłł had been dismissed from his post as Governor of Poznań – part of King Friedrich Wilhelm's policy of germanification of the Duchy, although he retained Antonin and still enjoyed the King's musical patronage; his recently completed opera, *Faust* – based on Goethe – was premiered in Berlin and continued to enjoy success for many years.

> *I've been giving Princess Wanda lessons. She is young, seventeen and pretty, it really was such a joy to guide her little fingers.*
>
> FRYDERYK CHOPIN to TYTUS WOYCIECHOWSKI,
> 14th November 1829.

On these occasions everyone sat round the piano to sing and play their way through *Faust*. Frycek was full of admiration for this remarkable and ambitious work. That year, inspired by the Prince's cello technique, Frycek tried his hand at chamber music; he wrote a glitzy *Polonaise brillante in C for Cello and Piano Op. 3*, for the Prince to play with Princess Wanda, and his *Piano Trio in G minor Op. 8* which he dedicated to Prince Radziwiłł.

> *I gratefully accept the dedication of your Trio which you are kind enough to offer to me... Accept, my dear Chopin, my reiterated assurances of the interest which your talent arouses in me, and of the high esteem in which I hold you.*
>
> Prince ANTONI RADZIWIŁŁ to FRYDERYK CHOPIN,
> 4th November 1829.

THE OLD TOWN SQUARE IN POZNAŃ

In **POZNAŃ** Frycek and Professor Jarocki had been invited to stay with the Archbishop, Teofil Wolicki, at his residence on the "holy island" of **OSTRÓW TUMSKI**. The Archbishop was a good friend – and a relative – of the Chopins. The next day Frycek called on Prince Radziwiłł at his official **GOVERNOR'S RESIDENCE**, the former **JESUIT COLLEGE** in the centre of the city. He was warmly wel-

The antique well in **THE OLD TOWN SQUARE IN POZNAŃ** ▶

A Journey to Vienna

O N JULY 22ND 1829, having completed his studies at the Warsaw Conservatory, Frycek and four travelling companions, University Professor Romuald Hube, classics teacher Ignacy Maciejowski, and old school friends Marceli Celiński and Alfons Brandt set off for Vienna. The first stop was CRACOW, which they reached after two days. At the Congress of Vienna, Poland's ancient capital and its immediate surrounds, were designated the Republic of Cracow. As a city steeped in history, the party spent several days there, sightseeing.

I was so taken with Cracow, that I could find very little time to think about home, or about you.

FRYDERYK CHOPIN TO TYTUS WOYCIECHOWSKI, 12th September 1829.

THE KOŚCIUSZKO HILL IN CRACOW. Chopin's father had fought under Kościuszko

There was much to see; the WAWEL, the ancient complex overlooking the RIVER VISTULA, incorporating the Royal Castle and the Cathedral, which was then a military barracks, the Tombs of Prince Józef Poniatowski and Tadeusz Kościuszko. There was also the newly completed, 300-foot high KOŚCIUSZKO'S MOUND, made of soil from his battle sites, including Maciejowice, where Frycek's father had fought under him. There was the MARKET SQUARE with the CLOTH HALL (SUKIENNICE) in the centre, dominated by the unidentical twin spires of the CHURCH OF ST. MARY (THE MARIACKI CHURCH); from the taller of the two, every hour, on the hour, a bugler sounded the *hejnał*, the aborted bugle call commemorating the bugler boy who warned the inhabitants of a Tartar attack 600 years previously, and died during its sounding.

Frycek had a chance to hear the local dance, the gentle, *polka*-like *krakowiak* on its home ground. He had been interested enough in its distinctive jogging rhythm the previous year to write a miniature piano concerto, considered by many as his finest work for piano and orchestra; the *Rondo à la Krakowiak* was published as Op. 14 in 1834.

98

The arcaded courtyard in **THE ROYAL CASTLE AT THE WAWEL**

THE SANDOMIERZ TOWER, one of the three defence towers at **THE WAWEL** ▶

Chopin's signature in **THE WIELICZKA SALT MINE'S** Visitors' Book, July 1829

The companions visited **WIELICZKA**, the oldest and biggest salt mine in the world, a subterranean fantasy-land of nine levels, incorporating 300 kilometres of tunnels, and signed the Visitors' Book. Among the sculptures and features was a **SANATORIUM** and **BLESSED KINGA'S CHAPEL**, all carved out of the salty rock.

Andantino quasi allegretto

Chopin's miniature piano concerto, the *Rondo à la Krakowiak, Op. 14*, is widely regarded as one of his finest works for piano and orchestra

The arcades of **THE CLOTH HALL** in the Market Square in **CRACOW** ▶

THE MARIACKI CHURCH in Cracow's Market Square

THE CHURCH OF ST. ANDREW in Cracow ▶

An old farmhouse in **THE OJCÓW NATIONAL PARK**

To the north west of Cracow is the valley of the **RIVER PRĄDNIK**, a tributary of the Vistula, traditionally the retreat of artists and kings. Perched spectacularly on a crag was the fourteenth-century **OJCÓW CASTLE**, once the imposing residence of the Counts Załuski; by the time of Frycek's visit it was already in the early stages of decline and dilapidation. On July 26th the party hired a peasant and his cart to take them to Ojców, intending to stay the night at the **HOSTELRY OF MR INDYK** in the nearby village of **PIESKOWA SKAŁA**. The expedition went awry, the driver got lost, was unable to cross the swiftly flowing, rock-strewn little river, and they all ended up stuck in the middle at nine o'clock in the evening.

About nine in the evening, when we were wandering around, not knowing what to do, we met two strangers, who took pity on us and offered to guide us to Indyk. We had to go on foot for about two miles in the wet among a mass of rocks and sharp stones and to keep crossing the stream on round logs, and all this in the dark night.

FRYDERYK CHOPIN to his family,
1st August 1829.

They eventually arrived at Mr Indyk's, cold and soaked through, but Mrs Indykowa, a good fire, a jug of wine and a sense of humour all saved the day.

THE CASTLE AT OJCÓW, to the north-west of **CRACOW** ▶

THE MANOR AT ŻYCHLIN where the wedding celebrations took place in September 1829

The next day the five tourists returned to their lodgings in the city. Just to the south of Cracow was the Austrian border, and the party crossed Moravia and reached Vienna on July 31st.

Frycek spent three weeks in the musical capital of Europe, during which he met a number of influential musicians and gave two very successful concerts which were highly praised in the press. With a reputation established and foundations for the future laid, Frycek and three of his companions – Romuald Hube had gone on to Italy – set off for home by way of PRAGUE, DRESDEN, WROCŁAW and KALISZ, where Frycek and his companions parted company; they continued on to Warsaw, while Frycek stayed with his friend Dr Adam Helbich, who had been invited to the wedding of Melania Bronikowska to Wiktor Kurnatowski. Dr Helbich suggested that Frycek should go as well. Melania lived at the Bronikowski Palace at ŻYCHLIN, just to the south of Konin, where the wedding was to take place. Konin was on Frycek's homeward route, so he accepted. It was a jolly, two-day affair, and Frycek joined in the fun and took active part in all the party games.

> *On my way home I attended the wedding of Miss Melasia Bronikowska; a beautiful child.*
>
> FRYDERYK CHOPIN to TYTUS WOYCIECHOWSKI,
> 12th September 1829.

On his return Frycek suffered a bout of depression. The threat of tuberculosis hovered over him constantly, he had a crisis of confidence in his musicianship. After Vienna he found Warsaw empty and provincial, Europe beckoned, but further revolution was in the air; there was unrest in Vienna, Paris and Milan, and even in Warsaw Count Novosiltsov's secret police were making more arrests than usual. Chopin's Poland was once more heading for revolution and disaster.

THE EVANGELICAL CHURCH IN ŻYCHLIN, where Chopin attended the wedding of Melania Bronikowska in September 1829, on his way home from Vienna ▶

Exile

OWARDS THE END OF 1830, after many months of agonising and indecision, Frycek finally decided to go to Vienna for the second time. Warsaw gave him a grand send-off; parties were arranged, and he called on all his friends, colleagues and teachers to say good-bye, even though he was not to know that he would not be coming back. Elsner, Karol Kurpiński and Karol Soliwa at the Conservatory, the Lindes at the Lyceum the Kolbergs, the Pruszaks in Marszałkowska Street, the Skarbeks, his friends the Wodzińskis, including his future fiancée, Maria, and Julian Fontana, who would edit his music after Chopin's death, and Moriolka. She and Frycek had been sweethearts for nearly a decade, and it was only in recent months that she had been seriously replaced in Frycek's affections by the beautiful singer, and Frycek's secret love, Konstancja Gładkowska.

The Romanza from the *Piano Concerto in E minor* was inspired by Chopin's secret love for the singer Konstancja Gładkowska

His closest friend and confidant, Tytus Woyciechowski, was not in Warsaw to see him off; he had to abort his studies to return to manage his estate at Poturzyn (near Lublin) the previous year, but when he learned of Frycek's plans to go to Vienna, he decided to go with him. Frycek was overjoyed at the prospect of having Tytus with him at such a critical time – the threshold of a musical career in greater Europe. Tytus was a fine pianist and an honest critic, and Frycek trusted and sought his opinion on his compositions.

A white stork's nest. A common view in the Polish countryside ▶

As Tytus would be coming from Poturzyn, the two young men arranged to meet in Kalisz at Dr Helbich's, and continue from there together.

> *When I have nothing to eat, you'll have to take me in at Poturzyn as a clerk; I will live above the stable, just as this year in the courtyard, and be so comfortable with you.*
>
> FRYDERYK CHOPIN to TYTUS WOYCIECHOWSKI,
> 18ᵗʰ September 1830.

On November 2ⁿᵈ Frycek set off from the Post Office at Kozia Street; in his luggage was a casket with a lock of Konstancja's hair, fashioned into a ring by Ludka, and a letter of introduction to the Russian Ambassador to Vienna, which had been given him by Grand Duke Constantine – and his now considerable musical output. At the toll gate at Warsaw's western approach at Wola, Frycek was met by Elsner and a choir come to bid him *bon voyage* with a farewell cantata that Elsner had written for the occasion.

The coach passed through SOCHACZEW, where the road to Żelazowa Wola turned off the main post route to Poznań. He had stayed in Sochaczew recently, specifically to visit and make music with General Piotr Szembek, who was in charge of the garrison, housed in the ancient Castle on the eastern banks of the RIVER BZURA. The General was a fine violinist who shared with Frycek a special passion for Paganini. The Garrison's band boasted some virtuoso brass players who impressed Frycek with their techniques.

> *It's all on trumpets; a kind called a bugle; you would not believe that they can do chromatic scales extremely fast, and diminuendo ascending.*
>
> FRYDERYK CHOPIN to TYTUS WOYCIECHOWSKI,
> 31ˢᵗ August 1830.

At KALISZ Frycek had a couple of days to spare before Tytus arrived. Dr Helbich tried to arrange a concert, but Frycek, put off by the abysmal orchestra, found an excuse not to become involved. When Tytus arrived, the two young men set off for WROCŁAW, where on November 6ᵗʰ they put up at the "Golden Goose". Frycek called on Josef Schnabel, the *kapellmeister* at the Cathedral of St. John the Baptist. Frycek had met him before, on Elsner's recommendation. Schnabel was particularly friendly towards Frycek, and could not do enough for him. He invited Frycek and Tytus to a rehearsal for a forthcoming concert. An amateur pianist by the name of Helwig was trying to come to grips with Moscheles' *Piano Concerto in E flat*. During a break, Schnabel asked Frycek to play; Frycek obliged with the last two movements of his *E minor Piano Concerto*. As a result the hapless Herr Helwig was instantly replaced in the programme; in place of the Moscheles Frycek would play his *E minor Concerto*.

Frycek and Tytus also met an amiable merchant by the name of Scharff, who insisted on playing host to the two young visitors. He took them sightseeing in a buggy, and invited them to a special musical function to which he had managed to acquire tickets. Herr Scharff was astounded to discover that Frycek was the star attraction at the function; it turned out to be Schnabel's concert, which took place at the MERCHANT'S HALL on November 9ᵗʰ. The next day the two friends continued through Dresden and Prague, and reached Vienna on November 23ʳᵈ.

Meanwhile unrest was growing in Warsaw. Talk in the cafés was of revolution and dissatisfaction with Russian rule. The Tsar's head of security, the hated Count Nicholas Novosiltsov, was arresting everyone suspected of activities against the state, and the prisons were filled to bursting with members of Patriotic Societies, artists and intellectuals.

Shortly after they had reached Vienna, word came of revolution in Poland. The Decembrist Plot to unseat the Tsar, which had germinated in Warsaw and had come to a head in St. Petersburg, had set off a chain reaction with the storming of the Belvedere Palace by insurrectionary forces led by an officer, Piotr Wysocki, on November 29th. After fifteen years of peace Warsaw was again ablaze. Tytus immediately returned to join the struggle, having advised Frycek to fight for Poland in the only way he could, with his music. Frycek agonised for many hours, then he too took a carriage back, but, after several stages, he realised the fulility of such an action, and returned to Vienna.

Poland enjoyed some short-lived successes, and on the 25th January 1831 Tsar Nicholas was deposed as King of Poland. A National Council, under Prince Czartoryski, was proclaimed, and Prince Michał Radziwiłł, younger brother of Prince Antoni, took Grand Duke Constantine's post as Commander-in-Chief of the Polish army. Utimately the Poles were no match for the numerically superior Russian forces. Warsaw was stormed, and the Tsar's retribution was terrible. The Congress Kingdom of Poland was annexed by Russia, and the suppression of the population was without mercy.

The enemy has reached my home! The suburbs are stormed – burnt down... Jaś, Wiluś, probably dead in the trenches... Oh, God, do you exist? You're there and you don't avenge it! How many more Russian crimes do you want? Moscow rules the world! I can only groan and suffer and pour out my despair on the piano.

FRYDERYK CHOPIN'S Notebook,
Stuttgart, September 1831.

Allegro con fuoco

Chopin's *Étude in C minor, Op. 12 No. 10,* known as the "Revolutionary",
was written in a rage against the invasion of his fatherland by the Russians

Trees protected from the frost by straw. A typical sight in the Polish winter landscape ▶

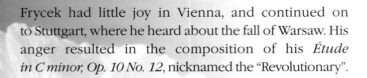

Frycek had little joy in Vienna, and continued on to Stuttgart, where he heard about the fall of Warsaw. His anger resulted in the composition of his *Étude in C minor, Op. 10 No. 12*, nicknamed the "Revolutionary".

Realising that his country was doomed, Frycek took the advice of many of his friends, and decided to fight for Poland in the best way he could, through his music. On the cold morning of the 2nd November 1830, when he and Tytus Woyciechowski had crossed

into Prussia at Biskupice, just south of Kalisz, he little realised that he would never see his homeland again. And so Frycek continued on to Paris, to a new life in a new world. Whatever fate the Russians would impose on their conquered land, Mazovia, the Kujawy, ancient Wielkopolska, Silesia, and the cities of Warsaw, Cracow, Toruń, Wrocław and Poznań would still live through his *Polonaises*, his *Mazurkas*, his *Grand Fantasy on Polish Airs* and the *Krakowiak*.

AFTER FRYDERYK CHOPIN'S DEATH Ludka Jędrzejewicz, née Chopin, brought her brother's heart back to WARSAW, where it was entombed in a pillar in the CHURCH OF THE HOLY CROSS, in Krakowskie Przedmieście. The plaque marks the pillar which to-day is permanently bedecked with flowers in homage to Poland's musical ambassador to the world.

The pillar in **THE CHURCH OF THE HOLY CROSS** where Chopin's heart is entombed. His body lies in the Cemetery of Père Lachaise in Paris ▶

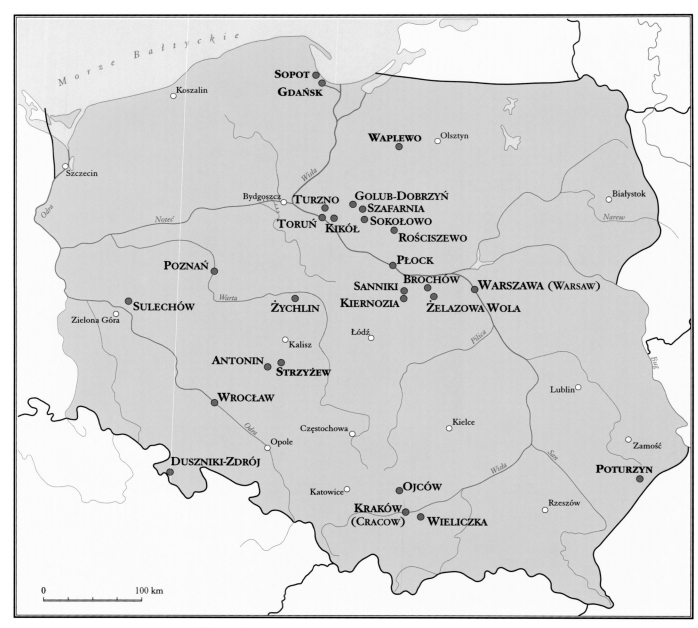

MAP OF PRESENT DAY POLAND WITH MARKED CHOPIN'S SITES

The map made by Wydawnictwo „Unicart" Sp. z o. o., Warsaw ▶

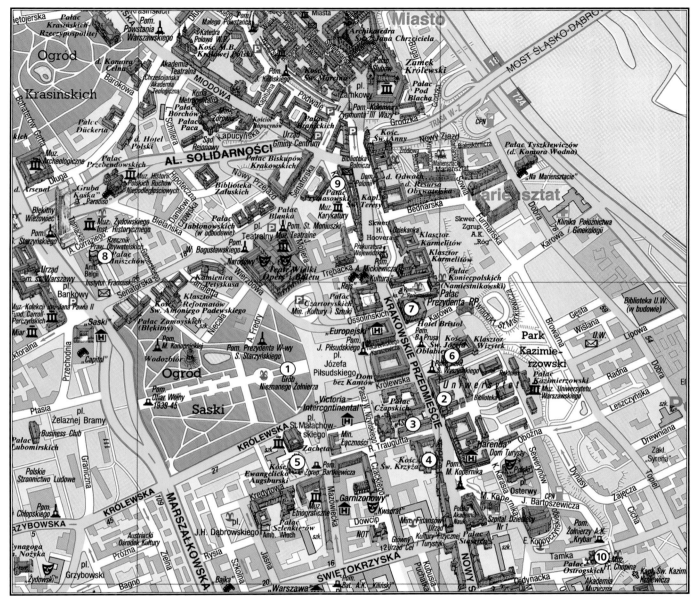

MAP OF CENTRAL WARSAW TO-DAY WITH MARKED CHOPIN'S SITES

1. **SITE OF SAXON PALACE** (presently monument to The Unknown Soldier) – Marshal Piłsudski Square

2. **CASIMIR PALACE** – The University, Krakowskie Przedmieście

3. **KRASIŃSKI PALACE** – Krakowskie Przedmieście

4. **CHURCH OF THE HOLY CROSS** – Krakowskie Przedmieście

5. **EVANGELICAL CHURCH** – Małachowski Square

6. **CHURCH OF THE VISITATION** – Krakowskie Przedmieście

7. **RADZIWIŁŁ PALACE** – Krakowskie Przedmieście

8. **MERCHANTS' HALL** – Senatorska Street, now Belgian Embassy

9. **SITE OF POST OFFICE AND TWO COFFEE HOUSES** – Kozia Street

10. **CHOPIN MUSEUM AT OSTROGSKI PALACE** – Okólnik Street

Index

Page numbers in *italic* denote photographs' captions.

Copy Editors

Irmina Wala-Pęgierska

Mary Pinińska

Technical Editor

Anna Kożurno-Królikowska

Production Co-ordinator

Wydawnictwo »JaR« Sp. z o.o., Warsaw

Music examples in Score

Sławomir Bychawski

All quotations translated by Pamela & Iwo Załuski;

translation of all fragments from correspondence of Fryderyk Chopin based on:

"Korespondencja Fryderyka Chopina", compiled and edited by B.E. Sydow, Warsaw 1955.